WILL THE REAL

CHURCH

PLEASE STAND UP!

A FIVE-FOLD MINISTRY LED CHURCH
The only AUTHENTIC MODEL for Today's
CHURCH!

How to MODEL and MOBILIZE Your
Church and Ministry into an
APOSTOLIC CENTRE!

Now Word Publishing, Salvation House, Unit 2 Sterling Court, Mundells, Welwyn Garden City, Hertfordshire, AL7 1FT

www.nowwordpublishing.co.uk

ISBN: 978-0-9929519-1-7

Cover Design: SFTN Media

Printed in the United Kingdom

CONTENTS

DEDICATION:

I wish to dedicate this book to the person who was my first and most influential mentor, not just in ministry but in manhood, my father, Kenneth Norman. His example of faith and uncompromising commitment to his family and to the church will forever be the example I will pursue. He was not only my father but my best friend. There was one phrase anyone who knew him would remember him for..."You've got to walk the talk!" This he did in every area of his life.

APPRECIATION:

I wish to thank the incredible people who are Salvation for the Nations International Churches for your commitment to pursue God's call to reformation with me. Thank you for your trust...thank you for your willingness to change and embrace new ways of thinking about and doing church! God has called us to do this - together! Thank you to my wife, Wyona and children, all of whom share in ministry with me. You are my A TEAM!

PROLOGUE:

Why have so many believers become disillusioned with church as we know it? Some of the reasons given are the church:

- Doesn't always appreciate my giftedness, my skill sets, or even my service to the church

- Doesn't always care about some of the things I value most

- Doesn't always offer the kind of support I need when I need it

- Turns my mistakes or grief into material for gossip

- Doesn't notice when I'm missing, sick or hurting

- Makes me feel judged, less-than or abandoned

- Gets caught up with the wrong priorities

- Is too inward focussed rather than outward focussed

- Makes bad decisions that end up discrediting or hurting the church

- Sometimes seems to ignore, misread, or misapply certain portions of Scripture

Why has the church become irrelevant in the thinking of so many? God's love is irresistible but the enemy has blinded their minds and in some cases even uses the church itself as a barrier. We have to face the challenges of reaching this post-modern, post-Christian generation! He has given us everything we need to reach the world. This is the time for the Church to respond and rise to the challenge of bringing the message of truth and redemption to the world in a relevant way that reaches right where people are and impacts every arena of our culture and society.

Jesus met people where they were at and was criticised for it (Matthew 9:11), but in so doing He demonstrated the Father's heart for the world that He so loved that He sent His Son (John 3:16). We are living in such an exciting time of incredible change with unprecedented opportunities to reach people for Christ! I believe that the reason why the world is no longer paying attention to the Church is because the Church is no longer paying attention to the mandate!

The Church has become so many other things other than what it was originally intended to be – An Apostolic Centre to change and redeem the world! This book is born out of my journey as a pastor and church planter and my quest to find the missing ingredients to authentic New Testament Church life. These principles will, I believe, enable you, to transform your church or ministry to one that will truly reflect God's original design for His Church!

CHAPTER 1:   GOD IS NOT FINISHED WITH THE CHURCH!

The Church is God's Plan:

The primary thing that we understand about the Church in the Bible is that it comes from God. It is not man's idea, but it originated in the heart and mind of God.

"To me, who am less than the least of all the saints, this grace was given, that I should preach among the Gentiles the unsearchable riches of Christ, [9] and to make all see what is the fellowship of the mystery, which from the beginning of the ages has been hidden in God who created all things through Jesus Christ; [10] to the intent that now the manifold wisdom of God might be made known by the church to the principalities and powers in the heavenly places, [11] according to the eternal purpose which He accomplished in Christ Jesus our Lord."
(Ephesians 3:8-11)

There are three foundational things that the Apostle Paul, by inspiration of the Holy Spirit, tells us about the Church here:

- The wisdom of God is made manifest in spiritual places through the Church.

- This was in accordance with God's eternal purpose for His Church.

- This was carried out through Jesus Christ.

Isn't that incredible to realise, that the Church was planned in the mind of God, before even the first star was created? The church today is the result of God's eternal plan and carries His eternal purpose. No other organization can make that claim!

The Church is God's Priority:

"And He put all things under His feet, and gave Him to be head over
all things to the church, [23] which is His body, the fullness of
Him who fills all in all."
(Ephesians 1:22, 23)

The Church is the Body of Christ and the "fullness of Him who fills all in all." This means that the Church is God's priority, or His goal. The Church is the main thing on God's agenda today!

The Church is God's Place of Reconciliation:

Reconciliation with God takes place in this Body; "... and that He might reconcile them both to God in one body through the cross, thereby putting to death the enmity" (Ephesians 2:16). The Bible is clear that in the redemptive plan of God the primary place of reconciliation with Him takes place within the Body – that is the physical Body of Christ and His Spiritual Body the Church, today!

The Church is Fore-Told in Prophecy:

There are many Old Testament prophesies about the Church that Jesus would one day establish. A quick overview of just a few of them should be sufficient to set the record straight: That the Church is crucial to our relationship with God and that the Church is God's priority on the earth today.

First that the Church, or Kingdom, would be open to all people of every nation, tribe and tongue, "Now it shall come to pass in the latter days That the mountain of the Lord's house Shall be established on the top of the mountains, And shall be exalted above the hills; And all nations shall flow to it" (Isaiah 2:2). In fulfilment of this prophecy, Jesus, in the Great commission, sent His disciples out to preach the Gospel to all the nations (Matthew 28:18-20).

That this Kingdom, or Church, would be established in Jerusalem, "Many people shall come and say, "Come, and let us go up to the mountain of the Lord, To the house of the God of Jacob; He will teach us His ways, And we shall walk in His paths." For out of Zion shall go forth the law, And the word of the Lord from Jerusalem" (Isaiah 2:3). Over seven hundred years later, Jesus told His disciples that they would see His Kingdom come with power and that they were to wait in Jerusalem for the promise to come to pass. It was fulfilled only ten days after His ascension on the day of Pentecost (Mark 9:1; Acts 1:6-8; 2:1-4; 30-31).

That the Church, or Kingdom, will not increase its territory through carnal warfare, "He shall judge between the nations, And rebuke many people; They shall beat their swords into plowshares, And their spears into pruning hooks; Nation shall not lift up sword against nation, Neither shall they learn war anymore" (Isaiah 2:4). When Jesus spoke to Pilate of the Kingdom, which He would establish, He said, "My kingdom is not of this world. If My kingdom were of this world, My servants would fight, so that I should not be delivered to the Jews; but now My kingdom is not from here" (John 18:36).

Finally, Daniel describes the Kingdom, or Church, as eternal, "And in the days of these kings the God of heaven will set up a kingdom which shall never be destroyed; and the kingdom shall not be left to other people; it shall break in pieces and consume all these kingdoms, and it shall stand forever" (Daniel 2:44).

The full significance of God's eternal purpose for the Church is pictured for us in the Book of Revelation. There we get a glimpse into heaven and what the triumphant Church is doing there. What will the glorified saints will be doing throughout eternity? They will be worshipping and glorifying the Lamb, praising Him and serving Him and even reigning with Him.

"And there shall be no more curse, but the throne of God and of the Lamb shall be in it, and His servants shall serve Him. [4] They shall see His face, and His name shall be on their foreheads. [5] There shall be no night there: They need no lamp nor light of the sun, for the Lord God gives the light. And they shall reign forever and ever."
(Revelation 22:3-5)

The Church is portrayed as His Bride, pure and spotless and clothed in fine linen (19:7-8). They live with Him eternally where there is no night, no tears, no sorrow, and no pain (21:4). That is the fullness of God's purpose; that is the reason the Church is His gift to His Son.

The Mission of the Church is Eternal:

We have to establish this biblical fact, that the origin of the Church is in eternity and its destination is eternity! The Church wasn't God's afterthought or "Plan B". The Godhead, the Trinity; the Father, the Son and the Holy Spirit purposed to bring about our redemption and the creation of the Church. How was this to be accomplished? Through the incarnation, the Word becoming flesh (John 1:14) and coming as the Lamb of God to take away our sin, (John 1:29) and make us righteous unto God, (2 Corinthians 5:21). And through the coming of the Holy Spirit at Pentecost to birth the Church and apply the finished work of redemption to God's people who would become His Ekklesia, His Called-Out Ones, His Bride (Acts 2:1-4; 40-47).

Jesus is the King of Kings and the Lord of Lords and He shall reign forever and ever (1 timothy 6:15; Revelation 1:5; 7:14; 11:15; 19:11-16). In His eternal reign, His Church, will rule and reign with Him, forever (Revelation 5:10). We have to get this revelation of the fact that the mandate of the Church is not a transient or temporary one. It did not begin in Old Testament typology and does not fulfil its purpose and use at the end of creation as we know it. Everything that the Church is and does counts forever! God's not done with the Church…He never will be!

There is a wave of revolution that is about to shake our world with local churches transitioning into Apostolic Centres based on the Ephesians 4 model and mandate!

CHAPTER 2:   THE CHURCH IS AN APOSTOLIC CENTRE:

What is an Apostolic Centre? First of all, an Apostolic Centre is a local church. It's a local church led by an Apostolic Team; consisting of the Offices of Apostle, prophet, Evangelist, Pastor and Teacher those who are chosen by the Lord and who are functioning in their individual Five-Fold Gifting or Ministry. The mission of an Apostolic Centre is to Welcome, Care, Train, Equip, and Send Out. The mandate of an Apostolic Centre is to see people come together to grow, get equipped, and go and manifest the Kingdom of God in their daily lives! An Apostolic Centre is built upon the Foundation of Apostles and Prophets (Ephesians 2:20-22).

The Apostolic Centre believes in, and is committed to, being a clear manifestation or demonstration of the Kingdom of God on earth. To accomplish this, an Apostolic Centre has a clear vision and strategy to extend God's Kingdom power and authority within the 7 Mountains of human society: Religion; Family; State or Government; Education or Educational System; Arts and Entertainment; Media; and Business.

Beyond simply believing in or preaching on the spiritual gifts, talents, and ministries of the Holy Spirit, an Apostolic Centre exemplifies a House of God, where various gifts and diverse ministries can successfully work together within the Body of Christ (1 Corinthians 12:1-31; Ephesians 4:4-12).

An Apostolic Centre is not just a gathering of people, nor is it a nostalgic looking back at the first century Church of the Book of Acts. Instead, it is a cutting edge, ground-breaking vision, bringing us back to our apostolic roots (Book of Acts), and then emerging in a contemporary and creative way, to continue the work that the first Apostles began and to do the greater works that Jesus promised we would do.

"Most assuredly, I say to you, he who believes in Me, the works that I do he will do also; and greater works than these he will do, because I go to My Father."
(John 14:12)

CHAPTER 3: WHY THE FIVE-FOLD MINISTRY IS ESSENTIAL IN TODAY'S CHURCH:

"[11] And He Himself gave some to be apostles, some prophets, some evangelists, and some pastors and teachers, [12] for the equipping of the saints for the work of ministry, for the edifying of the body of Christ, [13] till we all come to the unity of the faith and of the knowledge of the Son of God, to a perfect man, to the measure of the stature of the fullness of Christ; [14] that we should no longer be children, tossed to and fro and carried about with every wind of doctrine, by the trickery of men, in the cunning craftiness of deceitful plotting, [15] but, speaking the truth in love, may grow up in all things into Him who is the head—Christ— [16] from whom the whole body, joined and knit together by what every joint supplies, according to the effective working by which every part does its share, causes growth of the body for the edifying of itself in love."
(Ephesians 4:11-16)

- More than half of pastors feel inadequate to meet the demands of the job.

- The majority believe that pastoral ministry has had a negative and detrimental impact on their marriage and family.

- Many pastors claim to have experienced depression and/or burn-out to the point that they needed a leave of absence from ministry.

- An alarming number already felt burned out within their first five years of pastoral ministry.

There is no way to totally remove or deny the pressures that pastors, in their daily responsibilities, have to face. However, that pressure is greatly increased when the Five-Fold Ministry Gifts are not fully operating in churches today. It is therefore, of uttermost importance, to get a biblical understanding of the Five-Fold Ministry, so that we build healthy churches that operate according to the design and plan of God.

It was never God's purpose, for pastors to single-handedly carry the responsibility to equip and build up the Body of Christ. There is nothing in the Bible that even implies that any one senior church leader has been spiritually gifted with everything necessary to lead a particular congregation.

Five-Fold Ministers were never intended, so far as I can see, in Scripture, to operate independently of each other but according to God's design, are meant to cooperate in their special giftings and abilities, and together govern, guide, gather, ground and guard God's people.

CHAPTER 4: GOD'S FIVE-FOLD HAND OF MINISTRY:

"Therefore humble yourselves under the mighty hand of God..."
(1 Peter 5:6)

When Christ ascended to the right hand of the Father, He took His whole ministry mantle, divided it, and gave it in five parts to men and women. A person does not call or appoint himself/herself to any of the Five-Fold Ministries. It is a gift or calling of Christ Himself and, in time, is confirmed by other believers. Generally, a Five-Fold Minister has one initial primary calling and divine enablement to fully manifest one equipping gift. They may also have a secondary leaning in another Five-Fold area, and additionally, be called to manifest other Five-Fold Gifts at various times.

It is my conviction, as one looks at the function of the Apostles in Scripture, that those in The Apostolic Office can, as need requires, function in all five areas of gifting. A Pastor may mould his/her congregation to their own doctrines, beliefs and methods of ministry, but not into Christ's fullness. It takes all five Ascension Gifts working together to accomplish this. All five are needed to perfect, mature and equip the saints.

"Till we all come to the unity of the faith and of the knowledge of the Son of God, to a perfect man, to the measure of the stature of the fullness of Christ."
(Ephesians 4:13)

CHAPTER 5: THE CHURCH WILL NEVER FULLY FUNCTION AS A BODY UNTIL ACTIVATED BY THE FIVE-FOLD MINISTRY:

Scripture uses several different terms for the Church. It calls us a Flock of which Christ is the Shepherd (John 10:11). It calls us the Bride of which He is the Bridegroom (Revelation 21:9). It calls us the Branches of which He is the True Vine (John 15:1-8). It calls us Subjects of a Kingdom of which He is the King (Matthew 4:17). It calls us Children in a Family of which He is the Father (2 Corinthians 6:18). It calls us a House that He is building (Hebrews 3:6). It calls us a Temple He is indwelling (Ephesians 2:19-22). There are many metaphors for the Church. But one of them, and a very distinct and powerful one is the concept of the Body, that we are members of the Body of Christ (Ephesians 5:23-30).

The Bible declares that every believer is a member of the Body of Christ and every member of the Body has something to give. There are so many today that have separated themselves from the Body. They are not planted in the local church and therefore they will never fulfil their divine destiny. Any part of my body that is separated from the rest of my body will die. It does not have the to survive by itself. In the same way, if we are not vitally connected to the Body of Christ, we will die spiritually. There are many believers today who are spiritually dying and withering solely because they are not "plugged into" a local church body.

"I am the true vine, and My Father is the vinedresser. [2] Every branch in Me that does not bear fruit He takes away; and every branch that bears fruit He prunes, that it may bear more fruit. [3] You are already clean because of the word which I have spoken to you. [4] Abide in Me, and I in you. As the branch cannot bear fruit of itself, unless it abides in the vine, neither can you, unless you abide in Me. [5] "I am the vine, you are the branches. He who abides in Me, and I in him, bears much fruit; for without Me you can do nothing. [6] If anyone does not abide in Me, he is cast out as a branch and is withered; and they gather them and throw them into the fire, and they are burned. [7] If you abide in Me, and My words abide in you, you will ask what you desire, and it shall be done for you. [8] By this My Father is glorified, that you bear much fruit; so you will be My disciples."
(John 15:1-8)

I wonder if you noticed when you read this chapter how Jesus moves from the general to the specific. If you look at the opening verses of John 15, you will notice He talks about "every branch" and about the "branches". However, He hasn't gone very far when He begins to talk in terms of "I" and "YOU". It's very important to recognise that Jesus is not just talking about a general principle here.

He is looking His disciples in the eye and talking to each one of them personally and individually.

Just as Jesus did then, so the Holy Spirit does now! As I share this thought with   you...I am not just sharing a general principle of the Christian life, which may apply to some and not to others. But if you were the only person reading this, this is a word that Jesus would address to you! Because here, perhaps as nowhere else in the Scripture, we begin to feel as though there is nobody else around, it's just Jesus and me.

He says, "If you abide in Me and I in you...you will bear much fruit", and then Jesus makes this astounding statement, "For without Me (apart from Me) you can do nothing." Now that's very hard for us to accept! I know that there are many Christians who are not prepared to accept that principle. That's why there is such a deplorable lack of abiding! A lack of commitment, not only to God, but to the church where He has called us and to one another.

We have the mistaken idea, that we can function effectively, independent of God. We have the idea that we can function effectively, independent of one another. There are actually some Christians who have the idea that they can function effectively independent of the Church without submitting to leadership! Let me tell you, it doesn't matter what you think about it, there is no way that you can function, independently, or in isolation, as a Christian!

Jesus didn't say, "if a person doesn't abide in me...is not planted...is not connected to My Body," Because that is all implied here, He didn't say, "If a person doesn't abide in Me...they'll cease to function." He did say, however, that whatever you do, will add up to nothing in the sight of God...God won't recognise it...God won't regard it! You see we can burn ourselves out in spiritual activity but unless that activity is the fruit, is the outworking, the outflowing of our relationship with Jesus, of our relationship with His people, His church, it's going to count for nothing!

He said, "You did not choose Me, but I chose you" (verse 16). It is a fact that every one of us is chosen, regardless to the degree to which we may, or may not, understand it. Before you or I ever chose Him, before we ever had even that first notion of our need for Him, He chose us. He went on to say that He not only chose you, but He also, "appointed you that you should go and bear fruit, and that your fruit should remain." In other words it must be something that happens that grows out of your relationship with Him and that stands in your life, as a monument to the value of the choice that Jesus made in regard to you.

What kind of monument to Him stands in your life today? And for those of you who've been around for many years, or you've been involved and you feel now that you've done your part...have you ever seen a monument in a state of disrepair all crumbling and broken down?

"But now God has set the members, each one of them, in the body just as He pleased. [19] And if they were all one member, where would the body be? [20] But now indeed there are many members, yet one body. [21] And the eye cannot say to the hand, "I have no need of you"; nor again the head to the feet, "I have no need of you."
(1 Corinthians 12:18-21)

Paul is speaking here to the church at Corinth and he is emphasizing to them the fact that God has placed each of the members of that local church there for specific functions and everyone is needed. In fact, not only is every member needed but each member needs the other members to be able to grow, mature, develop and succeed. Your natural body is programmed to function with all of its parts. It cannot function without a heart, lungs or kidneys. Our natural bodies can stay alive without some of its body parts; however, it cannot function at full capacity!

Our bodies can live without our legs but our mobility will be restricted. Our bodies can survive without our hands but we will be handicapped. In the same way there are countless numbers of churches today that are surviving yet handicapped, because certain parts of that Body are not there or are not functioning! The Word of God declares that we are wonderfully made. God has made each of us with a unique gifting and ability. God didn't say that some of the joints have something and some have nothing. He said that every member has something to supply the church (Ephesians 4:16). So we have got to recognise that if we are not "supplying" what God has gifted us with, then the Body is lacking in that area.

Many look at themselves and say, "All this talk about reforming the church and taking the nation and impacting the city, is all well and good but what difference can I make? I don't think that I have anything to contribute that will make any difference! I'm not a pastor, I'm not an evangelist, I'm not even sure what my gifts and ministries are!"

"As each one has received a gift, minister it to one another, as good stewards of the manifold grace of God."
(1Peter 4:10)

As you look at that verse there are 3 principles that are clearly evident: Firstly, every member has a gift. Secondly, that we are to minister those gifts to others in the church. Thirdly, that we are to be good stewards of those gifts that He has bestowed on us. That's ultimately what we are going to be accountable for when we stand before God one day, whether we were good stewards of the gifts and ministries He gave us.

God wants to use us like we cannot imagine! He wants us to move beyond our past hurts and bad experiences and for us to start trusting Him to equip us as never before. He wants to use us but we have to offer Him something to work with. He chose us in spite of ourselves no matter what our shortcomings are or the insecurities or doubts we may have. He will even supernaturally make the changes, necessary in our lives, if we will allow Him.

God has given the Five-Fold Ministry the special responsibility, and the supernatural enabling, to transform churches from being "spiritual nurseries" to becoming equipping and commissioning centres. When the saints are equipped and released into ministry, we will see the Body of Christ rise up in unity and in the knowledge of the Son of God! We will rise to the full measure of Christ-likeness...and truly represent Him to our world!

CHAPTER 6:   A FIVE-FOLD MINISTRY CHURCH WHERE EVERY MEMBER IS A MINISTER:

"[16] Therefore, from now on, we regard no one according to the flesh. Even though we have known Christ according to the flesh, yet now we know Him thus no longer. [17] Therefore, if anyone is in Christ, he is a new creation; old things have passed away; behold, all things have become new. [18] Now all things are of God, who has reconciled us to Himself through Jesus Christ, and has given us the ministry of reconciliation, [19] that is, that God was in Christ reconciling the world to Himself, not imputing their trespasses to them, and has committed to us the word of reconciliation. [20] Now then, we are ambassadors for Christ, as though God were pleading through us: we implore you on Christ's behalf, be reconciled to God."
(1 Corinthians 5:16-20)

Every member of the Church is called, chosen and anointed by God to serve Him. He gives gifts and calls us all to the "ministry of reconciliation". Our local churches will never be successful in fulfilling their corporate vision until we grasp this and put (Ephesians 4:11-16) into practice. The Five-Fold Ministry Gifts were given to equip the saints for service and are to be active until that job is complete and the Body of Christ comes to maturity.

Five-Fold Ministries are divinely enabled to equip the saints to fulfil their ministry and purpose in the Body of Christ. The concept of part-time Christians led by professional clergy is totally foreign to Scripture. The Bible is clear - we are all in the ministry together! A distinctive feature of a Five-Fold Ministry Church is that every member is a minister - they know what their gifts and calling are and are equipped activated to serve in them!

It is an unfortunate reality that many churches have become Sunday "Spas" where believers are pampered without being trained and built up in the Spirit! If we are going to reach this generation, our local churches have to be transformed into places where believers are being raised up and released into their God-ordained ministries to serve, both in the church and in the world! It is by the power of the Holy Spirit that the Kingdom of God is advancing on this earth (Zechariah 4:6). There are dimensions of the Spirit's anointing which believers need for their calling in the marketplace, which the Five-Fold Ministry will also enable them to access.

When the Five-Fold Ministry is recognised and released to do this, every believer will be equipped with the Word of God, with the power of the Spirit, activated in the Gifts of the Spirit, flowing in miracles, signs and wonders - doing the work of the ministry! The Church will become the Army of the Lord, called, commissioned and deployed. While there will be captains and leaders, there will no longer need to be "one man show" ministries!

There are no insignificant ministries in the church. Some are visible and some are behind the scenes, but all are valuable.

Small or hidden ministries often make the biggest difference. Every ministry matters, because we are all dependent on each other to function. He created and designed you for ministry, a life of good works, which He has already prepared for you to do. "For we are His workmanship, created in Christ Jesus for good works, which God prepared beforehand that we should walk in them" (Ephesians 2:10). Once the saints are equipped they begin to minister. Once they begin to minister the Body gets built up, and when the body is built up the Kingdom is extended; lives, communities, nations are impacted! Now that's the true Church!

CHAPTER 7: THE WHOLE GODHEAD IS INVOLVED WITH THE FIVE-FOLD MINISTRY IN BUILDING AND BRINGING THE CHURCH TO MATURITY:

All the power and fullness of the Godhead is made available to the people of God to complete the task of coming into the fullness of the measure of Christ, the Bride ready for her Bridegroom (1 Corinthians 12:4-6).

- We have "diversities of gifts, but the same Spirit" - the Holy Spirit (1 Corinthians 12:4)

- We have "differences of ministries, but the same Lord" - the Son (1Corinthians 12:5)

- We have "diversities of operations, but the same God" - the Father (1 Corinthians 12:6)

- Christ Jesus gave Himself for the Church dying for her redemption - the Cross (Ephesians 5:25)

- He gave the Holy Spirit - the Day of Pentecost (Acts 2:1-4)

- He gave Gifts to perfect the Church and bring her to maturity - the Five-Fold Ministry (Ephesians 4:7-16)

These ministries are actually an extension of Jesus, Himself: His own ministry flowing into the many-membered Body of Christ. These ministries - the Apostle, Prophet, Evangelist, Pastor and Teacher are His instruments for the perfecting of the Church to represent Him on the earth. These gifts are incomplete by design, so that without each other we cannot fully express the nature and ministry of Christ.

CHAPTER 8: THE FIVE-FOLD MINISTRY CONTROVERSY:

When Jesus ascended, God created a new leadership model for the Church. There is considerable controversy in Christian circles today concerning the validity of the Five-fold ministry. Some maintain that the Five-Fold Ministry was only meant for the "Apostolic age" (30-90 AD). However, the Five-Fold Ministry did not pass away at the end of the first century, but was given until the maturing of the Body in unity, knowledge and expression of Christ's fullness.

One of the other major objections is that it supposedly creates an elite hierarchy of leadership. However, just the opposite is true. When properly understood, the Five-Fold Ministry in fact takes the emphasis away from a hierarchical leadership and places the weight of ministry towards a spread of responsibility across the church body.

The operation of these gifts, also sometimes called Equipping or Ascension Gifts, and how they fit together can better be understood through the analogy of how a physical hand functions.

CHAPTER 9:   FIVE-FOLD MINISTRY FUNCTIONS:

THE APOSTLE: THE THUMB

The thumb does not work in opposition to, or over the other fingers, but anatomically, it is designed to complete the full capability, function and strength of the hand. Apostles function in administration and (together with Prophets) lay the foundation by establishing proper doctrinal and spiritual structure, "Having been built on the foundation of the apostles and prophets, Jesus Christ Himself being the chief cornerstone" (Ephesians 2:20). Apostles operate primarily in the Gifts of Healing, Faith, Working of Miracles, Word of Wisdom, Discerning of Spirits, and (sometimes) Prophecy.

In today's Five-Fold Ministry church setting, they would oversee the development and sending out of apostolic teams. They would also participate in going to other cities, regions and nations to plant new churches; to assist existing churches in helping local pastors restore order and unity and to discern God-given strategies in order to extend their vision and territory.

THE PROPHET: THE FORE-FINGER

The forefinger is often used to give direction and so is usually called the pointer finger. This describes the main function of the Prophet. A Prophet operates in revelation and points the way for believers. We must understand that the Office of the Prophet is different than the Gift of Prophecy in that it carries a governmental authority and responsibility. The Ministry Gift of Prophecy is for edification, exhortation and comfort, whereas the Prophet flows in areas of guidance, instruction, rebuke, judgment and revelation or whatever Christ chooses to speak for the purification and perfection of His church. A Prophet is not just someone with a prophetic anointing, but a recognised ministry to the Body at large.

The Prophet operates best in teamwork with the Apostle. Paul (Apostle – Ephesians 1:1) and Silas (Prophet - Acts 15:32), for instance, co-laboured equally together in the establishing of the first New Testament church at Ephesus.

Because of the Complex and at times Contentious Issue of the Prophetic in Today's Church, the Following Clarification is Necessary:

There are three categories of Prophecy: The Word/Ministry of Prophecy – this level of the prophetic is limited to "strengthening, encouraging and comfort" (1 Corinthians 14:3; 31); the Spirit of Prophecy resting on or operating within or through a group (1 Samuel 10:10) and the Office of the Prophet (1 Corinthians 12:28-29). Scripturally, every believer is encouraged to move in words of prophecy, but only a Prophet should exercise the authority of predictive, directive and corrective prophecy, and even then only within clear protective guidelines.

Being part of the Five-Fold, Prophets also have the special anointing to be able to discern God's gifts and callings on people and to activate them into their ministries. Therefore, it is important to recognise that not everyone who prophesies is a Prophet, just as not everyone who moves in miracles is an Apostle.

In today's Five-Fold Ministry church, Prophets would oversee the development of trained prophetic teams to be able to give accurate and timely personal prophetic words, as well as form prophetic presbyteries or groups of ministers and elders who come together for the purpose of ministering prophetically to individuals or a church body.

THE EVANGELIST: THE MIDDLE FINGER

The middle finger extends the furthest on the hand and therefore it represents the outreach ministry extended to evangelize the world. Many limit the office of Evangelist to those who travel and hold mass crusades. However, whilst it certainly includes these ministries, the Evangelist is primarily the Lord's gift to the Church. The function of the Evangelist, therefore, is to equip and empower the church to evangelise!

A lot of people mistakenly conclude that the Five-Fold Evangelist's role is the same as that of Missionary. It is therefore important that we make a clear biblical distinction between the two. The Ministry Gift of Missionary is the distinctive ability to be able to minister effectively in cultures other than your own. It is the unique, God-given ability to effectively minister in a foreign culture for the purposes of establishing and/or strengthening the church within that cultural group. This not only includes other nations, but also potentially within your own city even neighbourhood.

In today's Five-Fold Ministry church, an Evangelist would oversee evangelism teams and outreach, and maintain passion and vision for winning souls.

THE PASTOR: THE RING FINGER

The ring finger is the wedding ring finger and this symbolises the pastor's commitment to his sheep, his flock. Whereas Prophets and Evangelists might come and go as they minister to the local and wider Body, the Pastor is committed to the local saints in a shepherding relationship. Bearing in mind, that because the Pastor is Five-Fold, this may include multiple congregations in a city wide ministry.

THE TEACHER: THE LITTLE FINGER

Although it's the smallest finger, the little finger is essential and provides balance. The Teacher grounds the church in truth through instruction in the principles of the Word of God. A Teacher is not just someone who teaches (we are all encouraged to teach - Colossians 3:16), but is a ministry which brings instruction to the Body at large.

Not all Pastors are Teachers – many love to preach and inspire the believers and while this is necessary, so also is the role of the Teacher to establish them on a solid spiritual foundation. While Prophets reveal the heart of God, Teachers reveal His mind. Prophets and Teachers balance each other in the church.

Prophets have revelation of hidden things in the future, while Teachers of the hidden things in the Word. Teachers reveal the specifics of the revealed truth, while Prophets reveal the spectrum. While Prophets possess foresight, Teachers have insight. And the list could go on...to reinforce their crucial function in the church.

CHAPTER 10: FOR THE SAKE OF CLARITY, A DEFINITION OF THE ROLES OF PASTOR, ELDER, OVERSEER/BISHOP AND DEACON:

The Ministry of Pastor:

A Pastor is not simply a leader over a local church, but has a Body-wide expression of ministry. As one of the Five-Fold Ministry, a Pastor is, more accurately a "pastor of pastors" or a "pastor of elders". A Pastor's emphasis in ministry is in relationship networking.

The Ministry of Elder, Overseer/Bishop:

An elder is simply someone older in the faith - a "father or mother in the Lord". An elder is not a particular type of ministry, but rather is a leader in the Body (1 Peter 5:1; 2 John 1; 3 John 1).

"The elders who are among you I exhort, I who am a fellow elder and a witness of the sufferings of Christ, and also a partaker of the glory that will be revealed: [2] Shepherd the flock of God which is among you, serving as overseers, not by compulsion but willingly, not for dishonest gain but eagerly."
(1 Peter 5:1-2) (see also Acts 20:17; 28-31)

The word "elder" - presbuteros - refers to any leadership ministry. An elder may be one of the Five or an "overseer" - episkopos – a presiding/lead elder over a local church, sometimes translated "bishop", "A bishop then must be blameless, the husband of one wife, temperate, sober-minded, of good behaviour, hospitable, able to teach;" (1 Timothy 3:2).

But whether a person is a Pastor (one of the Five-Fold Ministry) or an overseeing/lead elder (with pastoral charge of a local body - single or multiple campuses), both are called to be shepherds. Following the example of the Chief Shepherd (John 10:1-16), a shepherd's ministry is to feed (verse 9); protect (verse 12), guide (verses 3-4) and love (verse 15) the sheep.

Responsibilities:

- Support God's anointed (Acts 20:17; 36-38)

- Earnestly and willing tend the flock of God (1 Peter 5:1-4)

- Pray and anoint the sick (James 5:14-16)

- Rule, preach and teach (1 Timothy 5:17)

- Guard the flock of God (Acts 20:28; 29)

The Ministry of Deacon:

The Bible does not clearly lay out the function of deacons. However, on the basis of the pattern established in Acts 6, it would suggest the role of the deacon is mainly to serve. To do whatever is necessary in providing logistical and material support, to allow the elders to accomplish their God-given calling of shepherding and teaching the church.

Perhaps the most noticeable distinction between elders and deacons is that deacons do not need to be "able to teach" (1 Timothy 3:2). Deacons are called to "hold" to the faith with a clear conscience, but they are not called to "teach" that faith (1 Timothy 3:9). This suggests that the deacons do not have an official teaching role in the church.

Elders and Deacons Were Chosen Differently:

While Scripture does not provide us with detailed directions for the step by step procedure in selecting and appointing elders and deacons, we do have principles in the New Testament that govern the procedure. This does not involve a process of voting! Voting usually means the majority rule, which is scripturally wrong. The Kingdom is not a democracy, it is a monarchy, with Christ as the only King, Ruler and Lawmaker. Someone has said, "The first attempt at voting in scriptural matters marks the beginning of division: for and against." Voting for elders and deacons, with the majority vote winning the office, is not scriptural from any point of view.

- Those in the Five-Fold Office were chosen and appointed by Christ (Ephesians 4:11). That appointment comes ultimately from God through other Five-Fold Offices recognizing and affirming. We must always remember that a person's gift makes room for him/her (Proverbs 18:16).

- Elders were chosen by God and appointed by the Apostles (Acts 14:23; Titus 1:5).

- Deacons were chosen by believers and confirmed by the Apostles (Acts 6:1-7). That selection process may be by nomination or delegation or natural selection where a ministry leader naturally evolves into that role within an area of ministry and having met the biblical requirements is confirmed by the Apostles. All of the above roles and appointments must be within the biblical requirements of the New Testament: (1 Timothy 3:1-13; Titus 1:5-9)

"[5] For this reason I left you in Crete, that you should set in order the things that are lacking, and appoint elders in every city as I commanded you— [6] if a man is blameless, the husband of one wife, having faithful children not accused of dissipation or insubordination.[7] For a bishop must be blameless, as a steward of God, not self-willed, not quick-tempered, not given to wine, not violent, not greedy for money, [8] but hospitable, a lover of what is good, sober-minded, just, holy, self-controlled, [9] holding fast the faithful word as he has been taught, that he may be able, by sound doctrine, both to exhort

and convict those who contradict."
(Titus 1:5-9)

In reality, as believers, we should all be seeking to grow and mature in the Lord. The qualifications and standards of character, required of Elders and Deacons, are those which we all should be striving for, if we mean business with God. The realization of these goals of character training will have a direct bearing on the accomplishing of other goals that God has set for our lives.

"Not that I have already attained, or am already perfected; but I press on, that I may lay hold of that for which Christ Jesus has also laid hold of me. [13] Brethren, I do not count myself to have apprehended; but one thing I do, forgetting those things which are behind and reaching forward to those things which are ahead, [14] I press toward the goal for the prize of the upward call of God in ChristJesus.[15] Therefore let us, as many as are mature, have this mind; and if in anything you think otherwise, God will reveal even this to you."
(Philippians 3:12-15)

CHAPTER 11:   FIVE-FOLD CHURCH LEADERSHIP/GOVERNMENT:

It is my absolute conviction, born out of my understanding of Scripture that every local church should be led by a Five-Fold Ministry Team.

Essentially the Five-Fold Ministry establishes a team of leaders to manage or govern the church based on their giftedness in one of five areas, which together provide a holistic and balanced perspective to complete Christian ministry. This model is in contrast to the more traditional hierarchy church model with a senior pastor, associate and/or assistant pastors. It is highly unlikely to find all five streams of giftedness to be represented and well balanced in only one or two individuals, no matter how capable or competent they are.

The Five-Fold Model functions on the basis that leaders with the giftings of an Apostle, Prophet, Evangelist, Pastor and Teacher oversee ministry areas where they have a proven anointing to grow and edify the Church.

1.

Every Local Church Should Firstly Be Under the Oversight of an APOSTLE:

"[27] Now you are the body of Christ, and members individually. [28] And God has appointed these in the church: FIRST APOSTLES, second prophets, third teachers, after that miracles, then gifts of healings, helps, administrations, varieties tongues. [29] Are all apostles? Are all prophets? Are all teachers? Are all workers of miracles? [30] Do all have gifts of healings? Do all speak with tongues? Do all interpret? [31] But earnestly desire the best gifts. And yet I show you a more excellent way."
(1 Corinthians 12:27-31)

The Apostles are leaders and visionaries. They bring direction to the church. They have the courage and ability to keep the church moving forward, growing and building in new directions. Apostles are also "fathers", able to nurture and disciple the other ministry areas. I notice Paul here only mentions three of the five Five-fold Ministries, I believe this is because these three are possibly the most direction-giving to the local church, but certainly doesn't imply that the roles of the Pastor and Evangelist are any less strategic and necessary.

Where a local church Pastor is not functioning in the office of Apostle, it is imperative that he/she relates to an Apostle or is part of an Apostolic Network where that divine connection can operate. Unless there is that biblical order, a Pastor will never realize their full

God-given anointing and mandate and neither will the church that they lead.

Apostolic Preaching Distinct from Pastoral Preaching:

Apostles, Pastors and Elders all preach but the following distinctive between Apostolic Preaching and Pastoral Preaching brings a greater clarity to their function:

- Pastoral Preaching emphasises personal wholeness; Apostolic Preaching emphasises personal commitment.

- Pastoral Preaching emphasizes inward health; Apostolic Preaching emphasizes external purpose.

- Pastoral Preaching emphasizes our call to understand our true self and identity in Christ through contemplation; Apostolic Preaching emphasizes our commission to make Christ known, by changing our culture through societal transformation.

- Pastoral Preaching is necessary for a healthy church; Apostolic Preaching is essential for impacting the city.

- Pastoral Preaching emphasizes relational unity for the communion of the saints; Apostolic Preaching gathers the saints in unity to fulfil the Great Commission.

- Pastoral Preaching is inward-focussed and promotes care strategies for the sheep; Apostolic Preaching is outward-focused and promotes evangelism strategies for reaching the lost.

Both emphases are essential for today's church if it is to be the "Real Church" the Church of which Jesus spoke when He said, "On this rock I will build My church, and the gates of Hades shall not prevail against it. [19] And I will give you the keys of the kingdom of heaven, and whatever you bind on earth will be bound in heaven, and whatever you loose on earth will be loosed in heaven" (Matthew 16:18-19).

Therefore, whereas the Pastor is sent to counsel; the Apostle is sent to conquer. Whereas every person or church needs a Pastor; every people group or city needs an Apostle. Likewise, every Pastor needs an Apostolic Leader and every Apostolic Leader needs another one to pastor him/her.

Areas of Oversight:

It will take the anointing of the Apostle to break through and take certain spiritual and physical territories as well as maintain order and unity among the other leaders and ministries.

The Apostle trains, equips and raises up leaders/elders within the local church and within a wider network and enables them to increase their spiritual effectiveness and influence by providing spiritual covering, direction and accountability.

- Leads and coordinate the Apostolic Team (1 Corinthians 12:28; Ephesians 4:11)

- Governs the administrative operation of the church (2 Thessalonians 3:1-5)

- Pioneers new churches (1 Corinthians 9:2; 1 Corinthians 3:6)

- Grounds the church in truth (Colossians 1:25)

- Brings correction in erroneous ministry, preserves unity in the Body (1 Corinthians 3:3-5)

- Lays foundations in the church (1 Corinthians 3:10)

- Fathers new ministries (2 Timothy 1: 6)

- Has responsibilities to oversee ministries or groups of churches (1 Corinthians 4:14-21)

- A ministry of miracles, signs and wonders (2 Corinthians 12:12; Acts 2:43)

- A ministry of prayer and the ministry of the Word (Acts 6: 4)

- Laying on of hands for impartation of ministry (Acts 6:6), Imparts spiritual gifts (Romans 1:11)

- Marketplace Ministries/ 7 Mountains

Oversee those operating in New Testament Ministry/Gifts of:

Giving, Leadership, Faith, Healing, Miracles and Administration (Romans 12; 1 Corinthians 12)

2.

Every Ministry in the Local Church Should Regularly Be Seeking the Counsel of the PROPHET:

Prophets have a strong sense of right and wrong, but even more than that, they have a strong sense of the Holy Spirit's leading. Their spiritual antennae start quivering when things are going off balance or in wrong directions. Their voice is important for keeping the church on track in what the Lord wants to do.

Therefore, they have a voice into every area and department of the local church and should be consulted and their input respectfully considered. Their responsibility is also to train other prophetic ministries and gifts and establish proper protocols for accountability and biblical order in the congregation.

Possible Areas of Oversight:

- Watchmen Group/Intercessory Team

- Prophetic Prayer and Intercession

- Personal Prophetic Consultations

- Public Prophetic Ministry within the congregational gatherings – Sunday and other

- Prophetic Worship Development

- Marketplace Ministries/ 7 Mountains

Oversee those operating in New Testament Ministry/Gifts of:

Prophesy, Word of Wisdom, Word of Knowledge, Discerning of Spirits, Tongues and Interpretation of Tongues (Romans 12; 1 Corinthians 12)

3.

The TEACHER Establishes the Local Church in the Truth of the Word of God:

They will carry the main teaching responsibility within the local church. In addition to their teaching responsibility, they oversee all teaching, training and educational ministries and programmes within the church. They also oversee the developing and sourcing of training materials for use in the church. They train and equip others to teach and disciple.

Possible Areas of Oversight:

- Connect Groups

- Children's Church/Sunday School, Youth Church

- Bible College, online and Sunday evening

- New Believers and New Members Training

- Baptism Preparation

- Parenting Courses

- Biblical Financial Management Training

- Spiritual Gifts Training

Oversee those operating in New Testament Ministry/Gifts of:

Teaching and Exhortation (Romans 12)

4.

The PASTOR Preaches and Oversees all Pastoral Departments:

Those in the Office of Pastor preach, exhort and oversee all pastoral departments of a local church and assist the Apostolic Oversight in duties such as weddings, funerals, home visitations, prayer, counselling, and other ministerial capacities. In today's Five-Fold Ministry Church, a Pastor will lead and coordinate pastoral, practical and care ministry teams to ensure the well-being and unity of the flock.

Possible Areas of Oversight:

- Home and Hospital Visitation

- Counselling Ministries - Bereavement, Substance Abuse, Divorce Recovery; etc.

- Follow-Up and Discipling of New Believers

- Children, Youth, Young Adults, Mothers and Toddlers, Men's and Women's Ministries

- Practical Ministries

Oversee those operating in New Testament Ministry/Gifts of:

Helps/Service, Mercy, Celibacy, Hospitality and Martyrdom (Romans 12; 1 Corinthians 12; Miscellaneous Passages)

5.

The EVANGELIST Enables and Empowers the Local Church to Advance the Kingdom:

They advance the Gospel and in so doing they battle directly with the hindrances of the Gospel as well. There are many more warriors in an army than there are generals and so there must be those who operate in the Office of Evangelist in the church (2 Timothy 4:5; 1 Thessalonians 3: 2).

Possible Areas of Oversight:

- They will help every department to have an outward focus in evangelising the lost and extending the influence and reach of the ministry.

- Whilst the Pastor focusses on the needs of the congregation the Evangelist focusses on the needs of the community...they bridge the gap between the church and the community.

- They lead by establishing God-given strategies and initiatives for evangelism, outreach and soul winning for towns, cities and regions.

- They train and activate evangelism teams and the members of the church to be bold witnesses of the Lord.

- As a Five-Fold Ministry they also operate in signs and wonders or power evangelism and release others to do the same.

Oversee those operating in New Testament Ministry/Gifts of:

Missionary (Miscellaneous Passages)

CHAPTER 12: REFERENCE LIST OF SPIRITUAL GIFTS/MINISTRIES IN KEY BIBLE PASSAGES:

The main places in Scripture where we learn about Spiritual Gifts are:

- Romans 12 - Prophecy, Serving, Teaching, Encouragement, Giving, Leadership and Mercy

- 1 Corinthians 12 - Word of Wisdom, Word of Knowledge, Faith, Healing, Miracles, Prophecy, Distinguishing between Spirits, Speaking in Tongues and Interpreting Tongues

- Ephesians 4 - Apostle, Prophet, Evangelist, Pastor and Teacher

Some add the possibility of other Gifts:

- 1 Corinthians 7:1-9 - Celibacy

- 1 Corinthians 12:28 - Administration

- 1 Peter 4:9-10 - Hospitality

- 1 Corinthians 13:1-3 - Martyrdom

- Ephesians 3:6-8 - Missionary

- 1 Corinthians. 13:1-3 - Voluntary Poverty

- Ephesians 6:18 - Intercession / Prayer

- Luke 1:1-3 - Writing

- Psalm 33:1-3, Psalm 49:3, Colossians 3:16 - Music/Creative Arts

From Scripture, we learn the following key information about Spiritual Gifts:

- Every Believer has at least one Spiritual Gift (1 Peter 4:10)

- No one has all the Gifts (1 Corinthians 12:28-30)

- We cannot choose our Gifts; God does that for us (1 Corinthians 12:7-11)

- There is no Gift that every Christian possesses (1 Corinthians 12:29-30)

- Believers will have to give an account to the Lord as to how they use their Gifts (1 Peter 4:10)

- Spiritual Gifts indicate God's call and purpose for a Christian's life (Romans 12:2-8)

- Gifts exercised without the motivation of love do not accomplish God's intended purposes (1 Corinthians 13:1-3)

- Spiritual Gifts are for the common good to build up the Body of Christ (1 Corinthians 12:27)

Prophecy

The Gift that gives a believer the ability to proclaim the Word of God with clarity and to apply it fearlessly with a view to the strengthening, encouragement, and comfort of believers and the convincing of unbelievers. The special Gift whereby the Holy Spirit empowers certain Christians to interpret and apply God's revelation in a given situation. This Gift is distinct from the Five-Fold Office of Prophet.

Helps / Serving

The Gift that gives a believer the ability to work gladly behind the scenes. The ability to serve the church in a supporting role or to invest their talents in the life and ministry of other members of the Body enabling them to increase their effectiveness

Teaching

The Gift that gives a believer the ability to explain the truths of the Word of God clearly and to apply them effectively so that those taught understand and grow in their faith. This Gift is distinct from the Five-Fold Office of Teacher.

Encouragement

The Gift that gives a believer the ability to offer comfort, words of encouragement, hope, and reassurance to discouraged, weak, or troubled Christians in such a way that they are consoled and strengthened in their faith.

Giving
The Gift that gives a believer the ability to recognize God's blessings and to respond to it by generously, sacrificially, and cheerfully giving of their resources (time, talent, and treasure) without thought of return.

Leadership
The Gift that gives a believer the ability to set goals in accordance with God's purpose and to communicate these goals to others in such a way that they work together to accomplish them for the glory of God. This Gift is distinct from the Five-Fold Office of Apostle.

Mercy / Compassion
The Gift that gives a believer the ability to feel exceptional empathy and compassion for those who are suffering (physically, mentally, or emotionally) so as to feel genuine sympathy for their predicament, speaking words of compassion, but more so caring for them with acts of love that help alleviate their distress.

Word of Wisdom
The Gift that gives a believer the ability to sort through opinions, facts, and thoughts in order to determine what solution would be best for the individual believer or the church. This includes the ability to apply knowledge to life in such a way as to make spiritual truths relevant and practical in proper decision making and daily life situations.

Word of Knowledge

The Gift that gives a believer the ability to have supernatural knowledge and insight given directly by the Holy Spirit Himself, not by their own mind or their own intelligence levels.

Faith

The Gift that gives a believer the ability of extraordinary faith to be firmly persuaded of God's power and promises to accomplish His will and purpose and to display such a confidence in Him and His Word that circumstances and obstacles do not shake that conviction.

Healing

The Gift that gives a believer the ability to serve as a channel through whom it pleases Him to cure illness and restore health (physically, emotionally, mentally, or spiritually) apart from the use of natural means.

Miracles

The Gift that gives a believer the ability to serve as a channel through whom He pleases to perform acts of supernatural power that are recognized by others to have altered the ordinary course of nature and authenticated the divine commission.

Discernment / Distinguishing Spirits

The Gift that gives a believer the ability to know with assurance whether certain behaviour or teaching is from God, Satan, human error, or human power.

Tongues (Speaking)
The Gift that gives a believer the ability to speak in a language they have never learned or to communicate a message from God to His people. This may also include the ability to speak in a language not previously learned so unbelievers can hear God's message in their own tongue.

Tongues (Interpretation)
The Gift that gives a believer the ability to interpret the message of one who speaks in tongues.

Celibacy
The Gift that gives a believer the ability to voluntarily remain single without regret and with the ability to maintain control over sexual impulses so as to serve the Lord without distraction.

Administration
The Gift that gives a believer the ability to steer the Body of Christ toward the accomplishment of God-given goals and directives by planning, organizing, and supervising others. This Gift is distinct from the Five-Fold Office of Apostle.

Hospitality
The Gift that gives a believer the ability to provide an open home and warm welcome to those in need of food, lodging, and fellowship. It involves a readiness to invite strangers to your home (or church) for the sake of the Gospel.

Martyrdom

The Gift that gives a believer the ability to give over their life to suffer or to be put to death for the cause of Christ.

Missionary

The Gift that gives a believer the ability to minister whatever other Spiritual Gifts they have in another culture. This Gift is distinct from the Five-Fold Office of Evangelist.

Poverty (Voluntary)

The Gift the gives a believer the ability to purposely live an impoverished lifestyle to serve and aid others with their material resources.

Intercession / Prayer

The Gift that gives a believer the ability to intercede for extended periods of time on a regular basis and see frequent and specific answers to their prayers to a degree much greater than that which is expected of the average Christian.

Writing

The Gift that gives a believer the ability to express truth in written form that edifies, instructs and strengthens others.

Music/Creative Arts

The Gift that gives a believer the ability to present personal witness and inspiration to others through instrumental music, singing, dancing, drama or other creative expression.

CHAPTER 13: WHAT IF A LOCAL CHURCH DOES NOT HAVE A RESIDENT FIVE-FOLD MINISTRY IN ONE OR MORE AREAS?

If a local church does not have a resident Five-Fold Ministry in one or more areas, I would advise the following:

- Do not give people designations just because there is a need or management void.

- Five-Fold Ministries are not self-appointed but God-appointed and tested and approved by the Body of Christ.

- It is best to appoint a Ministry Co-ordinator to have oversight until the Lord raises someone up within the church in the Five-Fold Office.

- Where there is no Five-Fold Ministry to oversee, the resident Apostle is able, by virtue of gifting and anointing to fill that need.

- Where there is no one standing in the Apostolic Office the local church needs to consult with an Apostolic Network for their input and/or oversight.

CHAPTER 14: INDEPENDENT OR PARA-CHURCH MINISTRIES AND THEIR RELATIONSHIP TO THE FIVE-FOLD MINISTRY:

Independent ministries that have a wider reach than just the local church:

It is here, that we have to address the issue of ministries that operate outside of just the local church. Do they have a legitimate place and role within the Five-Fold Ministry Church? Are they biblical? This is an area that has been open to much misunderstanding and, unfortunately, abuse. There are those, who because they have had an unresolved issue within a church group or because they have an independent spirit that refuses to be accountable, just launch out on their own, to do their own thing.

There are also those, however, who have a legitimate call to a ministry that has a wider reach than just a local church and they too need the support and accountability of an Apostolic Team. Many have been misunderstood and even rejected by a local church which has caused much wounding for them and for those to whom they minister. We have to make a meaningful place of belonging and participation for these ministries. Their gifts and anointings are essential, if the church in the city, nation and world is to make its greatest impact!

Phillip for example in (Acts 6) was an Evangelist but related to the City Church in Jerusalem. He preached and performed miracles and there is also a record of his preaching in Samaria and baptising an Ethiopian man. In (Acts 8:14-15) the Apostles came following Phillip to lay hands on the people and baptise them in the Holy Spirit. We also read of Apollos in (Acts 18:24-28; Titus 3:13). His relationship was with the Apostle Paul as his oversight. He was an Evangelist and a Teacher and travelled to different churches throughout Crete.

Lydia was a wealthy business woman. She dealt with expensive fabrics. She was the first Christian convert in Europe and there is a record of Paul and Silas going to Lydia's house when leaving Philippi and Paul addressing the believers gathered in her house (Acts 16:13-15). Although the scripture doesn't expressly say it, it is believed that the trend in those times was for the owner of the house, where the church gathered, to be considered the leader of that church and related to the Apostolic Team.

Phoebe, mentioned in (Romans 16:1-2) was also a business woman and a deacon of the church at Cenchrea but also related to the Apostle Paul and had the responsibility of delivering Paul's letters to the various churches. There are so many who the Lord has and is raising up in para-church ministries who have had no Apostolic connection and support.

These ministries must be recognised and place made for them! I always suggest to such ministers that although their ministry may be para-church, they should always seek to have a relationship with a local church in the area they reside. Their ministry may not fall under that local church, but they need pastoral relationships and it is in a sense their "Jerusalem", where they can offer the local leadership support if they are willing or require it.

CHAPTER 15: WHAT DO FIVE- FOLD LEADERS NEED FROM AN APOSTOLIC NETWORK?

God has designed us so that we are dependent upon each other. None of us can do it alone. We need to realize how much we need each other. The pastor needs the evangelist to remind him we have a Great Commission that others must come to know Him. However the evangelist needs the pastor to remind him that getting them saved is not enough. We must disciple them. We must teach, feed and grow them. Both are necessary. We not only have a Great Commission but we also have a Great Command.

The prophet needs the teacher to say to him, "Can you show me that in the Word?" However, the teacher needs the prophet to say, "But what is on the heart of God for today? What is His current up to date Word for us?" Someone wisely said that a teacher without a prophet will soon dry up but a prophet without teacher would soon blow up!

A Network is an extended group of people with similar interests or concerns who interact and remain in informal contact for mutual assistance or support. This involves churches and/or individual ministries who have similar interests and seek to remain in contact (fellowship) with each other and therefore provide assistance and support. Apostolic Networks act much like a denomination but without the hierarchal demands and controlling rule of a corporate structure. The key elements and priorities are:

- **Like-minded Faith** - Those who agree on a core set of beliefs (Statement of Faith) and share a similar passion for advancing the Kingdom of God (Ephesians 4:13).

- **Fellowship** - To provide a meaningful place of connection, relationship and coherence for ministries, pastors and churches so that together, in Kingdom partnerships, we can reach our generation, shape our nation and change our world (Acts 2:42).

- **Prayer** - To provide prayer support recognising the power of agreement when we stand united in prayer (Matthew 18:19).

- **Training** - To provide materials and on-going training in Five-Fold-Ministry and other areas of ministry development. To stir up the gifts and bring revelation and impartation (1 Timothy 4:14-15; 2 Timothy 1:6; 2:15).

- **Covering** - Some network partners will request this and others not. It is a spiritual term for those seeking spiritual accountability through the umbrella of a spiritual covering. A spiritual covering is termed as the person and/or ministry someone relates to spiritually, is accountable to and seeks counsel from (Hebrews 13:17).

- **Validation** - To validate and celebrate the assignment and destiny God has called each of us to. It may include providing ordination credentials. This will be accomplished through licensing (for those seeking to be ordained but needing more time and training due to limited ministry experience at the present); ordination (for those currently ordained or licensed and seeking new ordination, also for those already currently active and serving in one of the various Five-Fold ministry gifts), (Acts 13:1-3).

CHAPTER 16: ESSENTIAL QUALITIES FOR APOSTOLIC MINISTRY:

What is ministry? "Ministry" is from the Greek word diakoneo, meaning "to serve" or douleuo, meaning "to serve as a slave." In the New Testament, ministry is understood as service to God and to other people in His Name. Jesus, by His example, set for us the pattern for Christian ministry, in that He came not to be served but to serve (Matthew 20:28; Mark 10:45; John 13:1-17).

Acts 6 gives us the biblical qualities required of those who were going to serve the Lord through ministering to the practical needs of widows. Those qualities, in essence, relate to all areas of ministry and are still just as applicable today as they were back then.

"Therefore, brethren, seek out from among you seven men of good reputation, full of the Holy Spirit and wisdom, whom we may appoint over this business."
(Acts 6:3)

1. Good Reputation/Honest Report (Acts 6:3):

"Having your conduct honorable among the Gentiles, that when they speak against you as evildoers, they may, by your good works which they observe, glorify God

in the day of visitation."
(1 Peter 2:12)

Those chosen had to have a good reputation. They had to have a good testimony amongst the people; be spoken well of with regard to honesty, character, actions, reputation. Most leaders don't realize that their reputation is an invisible force that affects every decision that involves them; how people listen to them and how fully people will commit to their vision and trust their direction

A person is also well respected because they are honest in speech. They are "not double-tongued" (1 Timothy 3:8). A person in ministry should be in control of their tongue. They also have a responsibility for being slow to anger (James 1:19). They are not a gossiper, talebearer or a slanderer (Proverbs 20:19). When we minister we are His representatives and so should follow the scriptural instruction, "Let no corrupt word proceed out of your mouth, but what is good for necessary edification, that it may impart grace to the hearers" (Ephesians 4:29).

It is so disappointing when one sees a lack of integrity and basic Christian ethics manifested amongst the Christian community. Leaders who don't keep their word or behave in a way that is not Christ-like when confronted with differing opinions. Even those who live duplicitous lives, without concern for how their bad testimony will affect the credibility of the church and the effectiveness of its witness! Remember, we should also have a good reputation both inside and outside the church (1 Timothy 3:7)!

Every person in ministry should, therefore, ask themselves the following personal questions:

- **Integrity Check:** How honest am I?

- **Reliability Check:** Can other people have confidence in my character and constancy?

- **Dependability Check:** Can I be relied upon to do what I promise?

2. Full of the Holy Spirit (Acts 6:3):

> "And do not be drunk with wine, in which is dissipation;
> but be filled with the Spirit."
> (Ephesians 5:18)

Before Jesus began His earthly ministry, He was anointed by the Holy Spirit (Matthew 3:16-17)) and came back from His wilderness experience, full of the Holy Spirit's power (Luke 4:1-14). Any one called by God to serve in any ministry must be filled with the Holy Spirit. He has been given to "lead and guide us into all truth" (John 16:13). Jesus instructed His disciples that they were not to begin their ministries/carry on His ministry until "they had been endued with power from on high" (Luke 24:49; Acts 1:8). The word "endued" means "to be clothed or to clothe oneself". A believer is not properly clothed/dressed for ministry until they are filled with the Holy Spirit!

The Bible teaches the importance and benefits of being filled with the Holy Spirit (John 16:12-16). Let us never underestimate the power and help that the Holy Spirit gives to us. Scripture says that He teaches us (John 14:26) and guides us into all the truth (John 16:12-15). He empowers us with the boldness to share our faith (Acts 1:8). He fills us with the Father's love (Romans 5:5) and the ability to have joy, peace, and hope (Romans 15:13). He helps us in the place of prayer and enables us to pray in the spirit and in alignment with the will of God (Romans 8:26; 1 Corinthians 2:9-10; 14:14-15). He gives us spiritual wisdom (1 Corinthians 2:13), makes us holy (1 Corinthians 3:16-17) and sanctifies us (1 Corinthians 6:11).

He makes us competent to minister (2 Corinthians 3:6) and gives us gifts and ministries (1 Corinthians 12:1-13). He enables us to walk in freedom (2 Corinthians 3:17) and continues to change and transform us (2 Corinthians 3:18). He enables us to display the nature of Christ and overcome the flesh (Galatians 5:16-26). He seals us unto God (Ephesians 1:3) and strengthens us (Ephesians 3:16). He guarantees our inheritance (2 Corinthians 5:5; Ephesians 2:13-14). He enables us to have; dreams, visions and to prophesy (Acts 2:17). The list could continue but I believe the point is made that we need to be continually filled with the Holy Spirit!

3. Full of Wisdom (Acts 6:3):

"But the wisdom that is from above is first pure, then peaceable, gentle, willing to yield, full of mercy and good fruits, without partiality and without hypocrisy."

(James 3:17)

The wisdom spoken of here is a heavenly wisdom. It comes from the Greek word "sophia" and this kind of wisdom is skilfulness in rightly applying the revelation of God that has been revealed to us so we can fulfil our calling in Him. It is the same wisdom that the Book of James speaks of. Every one of these fruits of spiritual wisdom that James mentions will continually be tested in Christian ministry!

If we are duplicitous and live impure lives, we will be discovered and disappoint people. If we are contentious rather than peaceable, we will separate and divide people. If we are harsh and heavy-handed rather than gentle, considerate and compassionate, trying to force our position and point of view, we will hurt and harm those God has sent us to lead. If we are inflexible, unable to submit or yield to God and others, then we will alienate people and become isolated and barren in our ministry. If we cannot show empathy and mercy to those who challenge and irritate us, then we will soon become legalistic and judgmental in our dealings with people.

This wisdom from above produces good fruits. It will be inevitable that we will be fruitful in our calling when we have God's heavenly wisdom operating in us and through us by the Holy Spirit, and we are committed to obeying, however He directs and leads us. The reality is that it is one thing to hear from God; but it is another thing to know how to apply what He says to us. That takes wisdom! Without this kind of wisdom, we will be unable to "walk the talk" and become hypocritical! Therefore, He said if we lack wisdom, we should ask the Father.

"My brethren, count it all joy when you fall into various
trials, [3] knowing that the testing of your faith produces
patience. [4] But let patience have its perfect work, that you may be
perfect and complete, lacking nothing.[5] If any of you lacks wisdom,
let him ask of God, who gives to all liberally and without reproach,
and it will be given to him. [6] But let him ask in faith, with no
doubting, for he who doubts is like a wave of the sea driven and
tossed by the wind. [7] For let not that man suppose that he will
receive anything from the Lord; [8] he is a double-minded man,
unstable in all his ways."
(James1:2-8)

Ministry is all about people and the "people business" is a challenging one. Someone has said, "If you ever find the perfect church, don't join it because you will spoil it!" I often tell those attending our new members' orientation class, "I promise that if you join this church, we will at some point offend you." Or, as someone else put it, "To dwell above with the saints we love, O that will be glory! But to dwell below with the saints we know, well, that's a different story!"

This heavenly wisdom gives us the insight and ability to be partial, in other words, not to be biased but to see people and accept them as they are. This is so important, especially when people we are ministering to, who often are in pain themselves, inadvertently and even intentionally hurt and offend us. We have to be quick to forgive and respond as Jesus Himself would. In our own ability, alone, this is all but impossible, but in His wisdom and enabling it is possible!

4. Full of Faith and the Holy Spirit (Acts 6:5):

> "And the saying pleased the whole multitude. And they chose Stephen, a man full of faith and the Holy Spirit."

How important is faith? It takes faith to even believe in Christ; it takes faith to believe that what God says is always right and true; and it takes faith to trust and walk in that each and every day. However, we are called as those who minister, to be "full of faith." The reality is, that if your faith doesn't continue to grow in your relationship with Christ, you won't have the faith to see God's Kingdom come not only in your life, but in the lives of those around you. Whatever faith you have inside of you will determine the outcome of the faith level you'll have for God at work around you. If you don't have faith for God to move, there's a good chance you won't be looking for anything to take place.

Unlike corporate or secular leaders, spiritual leaders do more than calculate, structure, and use available assets, they rely on God! Through their faith, they are able to reach beyond the resources at their disposal to access and take hold of the resources of God. Every great leader in the Bible had great faith in God. Abraham, Moses, David, Esther, Paul - they all excelled in faith. Everything Stephen did was marked by his reliance on God and the enabling and authority of the Holy Spirit. That's the way all Christians are to live their lives.

> "And Stephen, full of faith and power, did great wonders and signs among the people."
>
> (Acts 6:8)

CHAPTER 17: PLANTED IN YOUR PLACE OF ASSIGNMENT:

Many people today think that it's not really important "where" they go to church, just as long as they do! And I suppose the most important thing, is, that you "go" after all Hebrews 10:25 says..." not forsaking the assembling of ourselves together, as is the manner of some, but exhorting one another, and so much the more as you see the day approaching." But I believe that God has a higher purpose than just that you "go" to church...He has actually an ordained place for every person to be planted in his house grafted, connected into His Body!

Yes, God can use you wherever you are, but it is important to God that we are, in that ordained place, not another. The reason for that is because the Church, the Body of Christ, is meant to be not just a meeting place, a place of worship, a place of teaching and instruction, a place of witness to the world, but it is meant to be a place of divine connection! Divine connections only happen when God's people are positioned correctly in the Kingdom of God!

Your Assignment is always to a place!

You see, your assignment is always to a place! The New Testament believers understood that principle and it's something we have to get a fresh revelation of today. I believe, after years of working with; frustrated, floundering and fruitless people, that one of the primary reasons Christians don't succeed and are not seeing the abundance of God in their lives and in what they're doing, is because they are not in their place of assignment!

You remember, in Paul's instructions to the Church at Corinth, he said, "but now God has set the members, each one of them, in the body just as he pleased" (1 Corinthians 12:18). Once you discover your place in the Body of Christ - the place where He sets each member, then you find that you fit and you flow! If you try to sit where He didn't set you, then you will be "up-set" and upset everyone else around you!

The right people are waiting for you at the right place of assignment.

When Paul was moving in obedience to his new mandate after his encounter with the risen Lord on the Damascus road, Ananias was waiting for him at the house of Judas on Straight Street, just as the Lord had orchestrated (Acts 9:10-17). The right miracles always occur when you are at the right place. Remember the disciples when they encountered the storm in their place of assignment (John 6:15-20).

Prosperity and provision are always available when you are at the right place.

When Jesus sent the two disciples to find a colt on which He would ride into Jerusalem, they obediently fulfilled the assignment and the provision followed (Luke 19:29-35). Blessing and favour always flows toward you when you are at the right place. You remember when Isaac sowed in the time of famine and God had said he was to stay there and not leave. God prospered him in that place, against all the odds (Genesis 26).

"The righteous shall flourish like a palm tree, he shall grow like a cedar in lebanon.[13] those who are planted in the house of the lord shall flourish in the courts of our god. [14] they shall still bear fruit in old age; they shall be fresh and flourishing, [15] to declare that the lord is upright; he is my rock, and there is no unrighteousness in him."
(Psalm 92:12-15)

As we look at that we can see the desire and will of the Lord clearly stated, His desire is for his people to be planted in His House. The House of the Lord that the psalmist refers to is a physical place of worship. The House of the Lord is what we now refer to...as the local church.

God desires for His people to be "planted" in a local church!

I actually had someone say to me, "We're just not church people... We're Christians but we just don't like church!" Then there are those who would say that the church has just become a man-made institution and is not fulfilling the mandate that Jesus gave it, "Therefore, I'll just separate myself from it!" But who gave you permission to do that? Jesus certainly didn't!

The Greek word for "church" is "ekklesia" and it means a "calling out" and an "assembly". You see we've got to get this right in our thinking. You, by yourself, are a member of the Body of Christ, that's biblical, without question! But when the members assemble together we have the church! And the Bible says that those who are "planted" will flourish.

"blessed is the man who walks not in the counsel of the ungodly, nor stands in the path of sinners, nor sits in the seat of the scornful

2 but his delight is in the law of the lord, and in his law he meditates day and night. 3 he shall be like a tree planted by the rivers of water, that brings forth its fruit in its season, whose leaf also shall not wither; and whatever he does shall prosper."
(Psalm 1:1-3)

I believe that one of the primary reasons today why many believers, who know the Word of God, who know the promises of God, are not living and walking in that reality, is because they are not planted, and indeed because they refuse to be planted, in the local church. In the many years that I've been a pastor, I've seen it many times, that people who are not planted are like trees with no fruit. They can be saying all the right things, but there's no fruit! They can be believing all the right things, but there's no fruit! Their ministries can be doing all the right things, but there's no fruit!

Now understand this that since we are living in the Church Age, when the Holy Spirit has been poured out and He indwells every believer, and we have the Five-Fold Ministry and the Gifts of the Holy Spirit are operating and the Ministry/Motivational Gifts are operating in the Body of Christ - your place of assignment is firstly and fore-mostly your local church!

Everything in the New Testament was centred on and flowed from the church!

When we get saved, God doesn't just call us to Himself, but He also calls us to one another! He says," Love the Lord your God and then love your neighbour as yourself" (Luke 10:27). Everything about the New Testament Church was about relationship, community, belonging, loving, sharing, caring - a Body, a House, a Family...it's always together! In the New Testament you will constantly find this phrase, "one another", love one another, share with one another, encourage one another, forgive one another, bear one another's burdens, pray for one another. I call it the "one another principle".

It simply means that there are some needs in your life that will not be met except by God working through somebody else!

We see that principle at work over and over in the Bible - Some of them will be your **introducers**, helping you to find your place, introducing you to the opportunities God has scheduled for you. Some of them will be your **ladder** to your next level. Some will be your **challenge**, to provoke you to develop yourself and bring out the best in you! Some will be your **friends** and **covenant partners**. You need them when you are starting to tire. They will help rekindle the fire in you!

The fact is, that when you are in your place of assignment – everybody that you come in contact with has something to do with your destiny!

There are things in life you may never have, until somebody comes into your life and gives them to you! There are places you may never go, until somebody comes into your life and takes you there! There are things you may never know, until you meet the right person and they show you! Tell yourself..."I've got to be planted in my place of assignment!"

There is much more I could say and many more pages I could write, but if what I have already highlighted does not convince someone that being a member of the Church, Jesus' Body, is an indispensable part of their relationship with God, then they are likely to remain unconvinced until the final day when Jesus presents His Church to the Father, and they are not a part of it!

"Christ also loved the church and gave Himself for her, [26] that He might sanctify and cleanse her with the washing of water by the

word, ²⁷ that He might present her to Himself a glorious church, not
having spot or wrinkle or any such thing, but that she
should be holy and without blemish."
(Ephesians 5:25-27)

"He handed out gifts above and below, filled heaven with his gifts, filled earth with his gifts. He handed out gifts of apostle, prophet, evangelist, and pastor-teacher to train Christ's followers in skilled servant work, working within Christ's body, the church, until we're all moving rhythmically and easily with each other, efficient and graceful in response to God's Son, fully mature adults, fully developed within and without, fully alive like Christ. No prolonged infancies among us, please. We'll not tolerate babes in the woods, small children who are an easy mark for impostors. God wants us to grow up, to know the whole truth and tell it in love—like Christ in everything. We take our lead from Christ, who is the source of everything we do. He keeps us in step with each other. His very breath and blood flow through us, nourishing us so that we will grow up healthy in God, robust in love."

THE MESSAGE

THE MANDATE OF REFORMATION3 NETWORK
OF MINISTRIES & CHURCHES

We believe God has called us to help shape and model a significant shift in the Church; how the Church sees the Church, how the world sees the Church and how the Church functions and operates. This shift will see it break free from many of the man-made religious, unbiblical models and structures, that particularly in the context of Europe and the western world have caused it to lose ground, lose relevance, lose credibility and momentum!

We've seen groups, that have rightly discerned what is lacking in the church, spring up and they've become almost sectarian. Why? - Because they've become disconnected from the local church. Why? Because the church hasn't made room for them! But that is the role of the church; that's what the church should be doing!

Part of the function, I believe, of our REFORMATION3 NETWORK OF MINISTRIES & CHURCHES is to provide a meaningful place of connection, relationship and coherence for ministries, pastors and churches so that together, in Kingdom partnerships, we can reach our generation, shape our nation and change our world!

Please visit our website for more information on how you can connect with us and the teaching and training events and materials that are available: www.reformation3.com

ABOUT DR BRAD NORMAN:

Dr Brad Norman is a biblical academic, pastor, teacher, visionary, mentor and motivational speaker. He preaches a real and relevant word with a strong apostolic emphasis. He holds a Seminary Diploma in Divinity, a Bachelors in Theology, Masters in Biblical Studies and a Doctor of Ministry degree. In addition to pastoral ministry, he has served on the faculty of two theological colleges, lecturing in Systematic Theology and Pastoral Ethics.

His message of 'Enlightened Empowerment' and 'Present-Day Truth' has brought invitations for him to minister in many nations, in conferences and leadership training events. Throughout his 25 years in Ministry, Brad has sustained a spirit of excellence and integrity. He is passionate not only to see believers equipped and local churches mobilized in their mandate and mission, but also for leaders and pastors serving on the front-line.

He was born in Durban, South Africa and raised up under his spiritual parents, Dr Fred and Ps Nellie Roberts. After relocating to the United Kingdom in 2000, he has been instrumental in the successful establishing of several churches under the covering of SALVATION FOR THE NATIONS INTERNATIONAL CHURCHES which he, together with his wife, Wyona, established in the January of 2003.

Since then they have been sought out by many churches, church leaders and pastors who are seeking relationship and apostolic partnership. This has led to the establishing of REFORMATION3 NETWORK OF MINISTRIES & CHURCHES; which offers ministry accreditation, as well as training and mentoring programmes seeking to restore a true biblical model for a fully functional Five-fold Ministry in the church today. The online REFORMATION3 COLLEGE OF MINISTRY & LEADERSHIP offers a 1st Year - Certificate in Biblical Studies, a 2nd Year - Diploma in Ministry and a 3rd Year - Bachelor of Ministry Degree programme. Visit the college at: www.reformation3college.com

Brad and Wyona live in Hertfordshire, Greater London, where they have their ministry headquarters and conference centre; Salvation House. They have a son, Devon and a daughter, Bianca. In addition they have two adopted children; Tia and Bella who are possibly the most spoilt Bichon puppies in the world! For more details and information on their itinerary or how to invite them to speak at your conference or church event please visit the ministry website.

ANOTHER INSPIRING BOOK BY DR BRAD NORMAN:

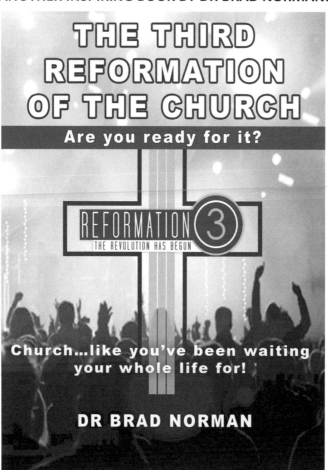

Hezekiah = 20   2 Kings 20:5-6
Isaiah visits hi